# Google Classroom
The Ultimate Guide to Learn Google Classroom Fast (2016 Updated User Guide, Google Guide, Google Classrooms, Google Drive, Google Apps, tips and tricks)

STEVE JACOBS

Copyright © 2016 Steve Jacobs

All rights reserved.

ISBN: 1539025748

ISBN-13: 978-1539025740

# CONTENTS

Introduction .................................................................................................. 4

Chapter 1 – The Digital Classroom Advantage ......................................... 7

Chapter 2 – Getting Started ..................................................................... 11

Chapter 3 – Practical Applications .......................................................... 23

Chapter 4 – Special Features ................................................................... 29

Conclusion ................................................................................................ 34

# Introduction

*Why Go Digital?*

Google Classroom is the future of teaching; consolidating class assignments, curriculum, and school announcements, this application not only eliminates paperwork, but also allows parents and teachers to stay connected from home within a single database.

Schools enrolled in the Google Apps for Education (GAFE) program have access to Google Classroom, along with parents, guardians, and students. Teaching professionals are able to upload reports, work assignments, and grades directly to the application where it can be shared and viewed by other members.

Imagine a child has missed several days of school due to illness; parents can simply check in with the teacher and prevent the child from falling behind in classwork as well as homework. Having mobile access allows families, additionally, to access content on vacation, or over holiday breaks.

Among other timewise and cost-saving advantages, Google Classroom provides shared email, collaborative learning, waste elimination, and more efficient communication than ever before. This application has revolutionized the lives of teaching professionals and administration, and raised the bar for educational systems globally.

*Where To Begin*

In this easy-to-follow manual for teachers, you will learn how to initially set-up a Google Classroom account and personalize every aspect of your digital classroom. The various features that set Google Classroom apart from other consolidating databases are described in chapter one. It is important for teaching professionals to get acquainted with the wide-range of applications, customization, and tools they now have at their disposal.

Additionally, computer terminology and acronyms are explained here with some detail to make everything easier to digest for people who may not have as much experience with computer systems such as Google Classroom. Fortunately, Google Classroom was specifically designed to be easily accessible for new users, and grade school-aged students. It really is a walk in the digital park!

*Learning the Ropes*

In chapter two, the step-by-step process of initializing your GAFE account and building a digital classroom are described in detail. Basic start-up instructions are provided for everyday uses such as starting new classes, inviting students, uploading files, using Google Calendar, creating assignments, and posting grades.

Chapter three provides additional tutorials for ways to customize your classrooms and organize your data most efficiently. Applications such as posting announcements, creating and saving drafts for future homework assignments, sharing documents with students, editing posts, and uploading audio, video, and photo documents to class posts are described in detail here. Privacy and permission filters are also explained in this chapter.

There are, of course, additional features of the Google Classroom that are less commonly used, but equally important to have a basic understanding of, as a teaching professional in the digital age. These features are outlined and briefly explained in chapter four. They include sharing data across various Google Applications, taking and posting pictures through Google Classroom directly, and creating student summary emails to which parents and guardians may subscribe.

# Chapter 1 – The Digital Classroom Advantage

The Google Classroom application offers a revolutionary solution to classroom management with a wide range of features that enhances the work of teaching professionals every day. A digital classroom practically eliminates paperwork, consolidates record keeping for multiple classes, and simplifies communication with students, parents, and administration. These features allow teachers to focus more of their attention on the work that matters most: education.

Teachers and administration who have made the switch to utilizing digital classrooms choose Google Classroom because it is easy to use, synchronizes applications (Gmail, Drive, Calendars, Docs, Forms), and it is completely secure and ad-free.

Information security is of utmost importance in the technological age. Google will never use your personal content or students' information for advertising purposes, and the application itself is free, without advertisement pop-ups crowding your classroom dashboard. You and your students can focus on work without worrying about distractions or security threats. Google Classroom has everything under control.

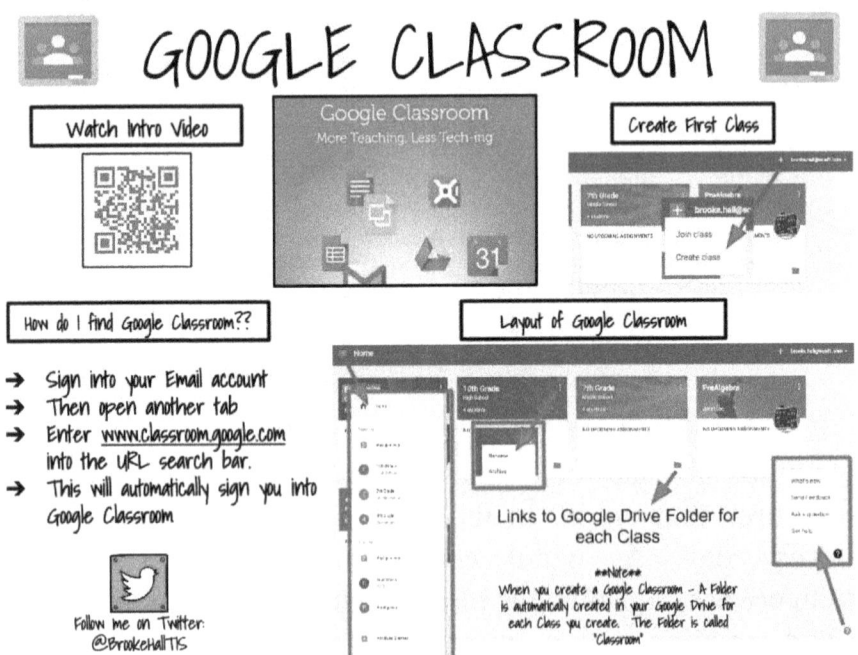

GOOGLE CLASSROOM

*Digital Is Better*

Teachers, students, and parents can connect online in a way that makes communication more efficient, clear, and time-wise. Appointments and assignment due dates can be scheduled with ease via Google Calendar so that everyone is on the same page, eliminating misinformation and making it practically impossible for students to fall behind in the event of missed schooling.

Google Calendar events remind students when an assignment is coming up due. Additionally, teachers can see if students have yet to begin working on an assignment. There is no room for the old "dog ate my homework" excuse. Google Classroom provides a system of accountability to help students better manage their time and set them up for success.

Filing cabinets and datebooks are officially a thing of the past. With Google Classroom, students can download assignment files and edit them on their personal computers, or in the computer lab, without ever having to print a hardcopy. Teachers can save files in digital storage space and provide any comments or feedback for students directly on the word processing document. There is hardly a need for paper and pens in a Google Classroom.

Grades can be posted and shared with students almost instantly. Teachers can also share grades and progress reports with parents by simply adjusting privacy settings to allow sharing capabilities. Students will no longer be responsible for bringing home report cards. Teachers and parents have a direct line of communication through Google Classroom now.

## *Information at Your Fingertips*

Having access to the world wide web of information is an

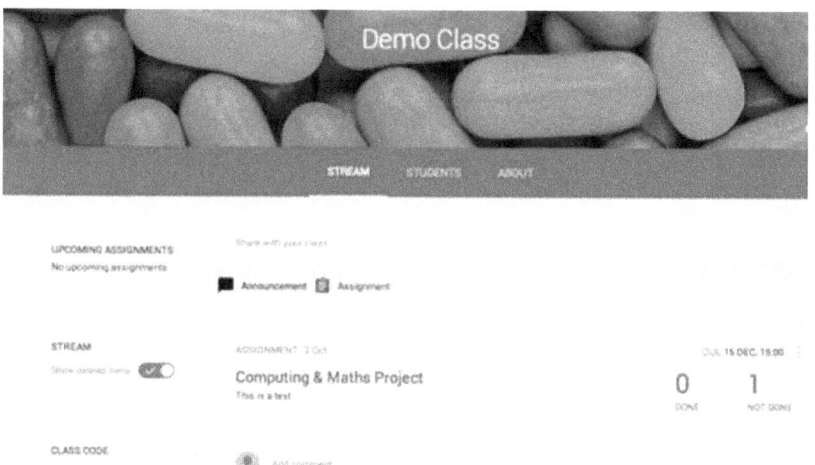

advantage that no longer requires the aid of various technologies such as televisions, video players, or projectors in the classroom. Teachers have the ability to post videos and share other visual content such as charts, graphs, and hyperlinks to educational websites on the classroom stream, where students can view them from home. This alone eliminates wasted time in class and makes it much easier for teachers to manage classroom activities.

What Comes Next?

In the following chapters we will discuss how to use Google Classroom most efficiently and take a closer look at features such as digital assignment posting, multi-class announcements, synchronizing email and classroom lists, sharing content across various applications, uploading files, sharing videos, adding and maintaining classroom roster, and personalizing classroom dashboards.

# Chapter 2 – Getting Started

*Logging In*

There are two ways to initially launch Google Classroom online. You can launch Google Chrome (classroom.google.com) and sign-in to Google Accounts with your school Gmail address and password (through the school's GAFE domain). The second option is to open the Google Play web-store and install the free Google Classroom application and create a shortcut for your desktop with auto sign-in capabilities.

There are two ways to get to Google Classroom.

- Go to https://classroom.google.com

- Go to https://www.google.com/
    - Click on the App menu icon
        - Select classroom

Once you have successfully opened Google Classroom, the homepage will provide two options for signing into and accessing the Dashboard (the options being teacher and student). From here you will select "I am a teacher" which will give you the ability to customize and maintain the Classroom Dashboard according to your preferences.

*Teacher Profile*

As a teacher, and administrative contributor to the class homepage, you have the option to upload and set a profile picture. This photo, if you choose to display one, will appear next to your name in the classroom stream and on the "Class Card" which appears on the home screen, or dashboard.

Google Classroom uses your Google profile picture by default, if you enable the photo display option. To change the existing picture, or to upload a new one, you will need to open your Gmail account. In the top-right corner, select the "Settings" tab, as symbolized by a small cog. You will see a

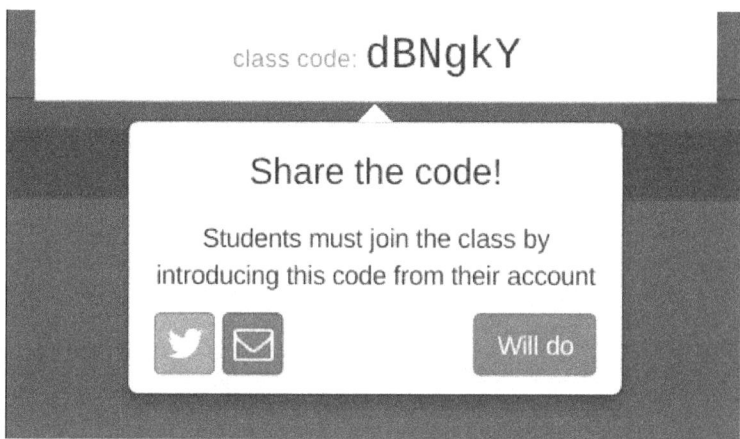

section on the Settings screen labeled "My Picture," and beside it, an option to "Change Picture."

From here you can either change or upload a picture from Google Drive. You will have the option to crop the selected photo and preview how the profile picture will appear to viewers. Once you are content with your selection, be sure to click "Apply Changes" to ensure that your updated photo has been saved.

*Creating Classes*

The next step is to create a class. To do this, you will select the plus-sign on the dashboard, or classroom homepage, sometimes referred to as the "stream." This button is symbolized as a "+" on the "Classes" tab. After clicking the "+" you will be prompted to create a title.

You will also have the opportunity to provide a description for the class, where you can include a class code, room number, and any other relevant information for the particular class.

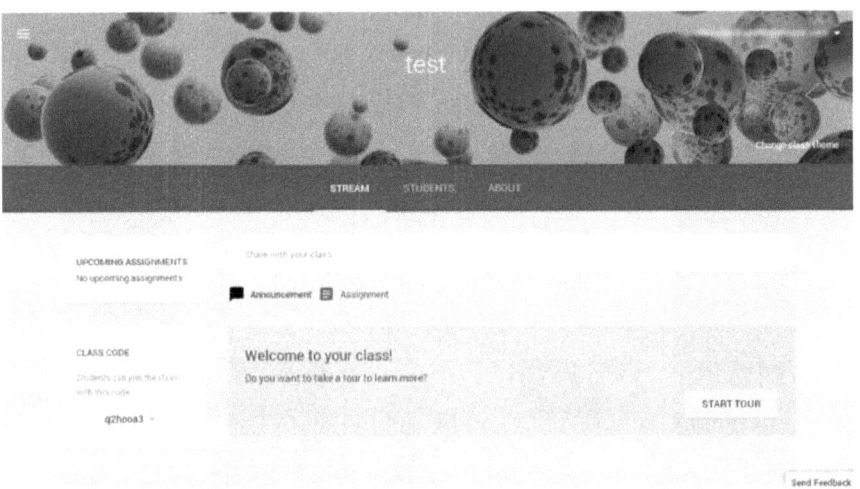

Next you will have the option to select a decorative banner which may help you identify and differentiate one class from the next. There are several different banner images to choose from on Google Classroom. The option, of course, is completely preferential.

*Inviting Students*

Once the class has been created you will need to add students. There are two ways to complete this task. Both are perfectly viable options, and depends entirely on the teacher's personal preference. The first option is to create a unique class code which allow students to join your class. The alternative option is to manually invite students to the class through their student email accounts.

*Option 1: Class Code*

To create a class code you will select the "Reset" option under the class code, which will generate an original code that exists only for that specific class. That code can then be given to students and they will simply search for the class by its code and select the option to join.

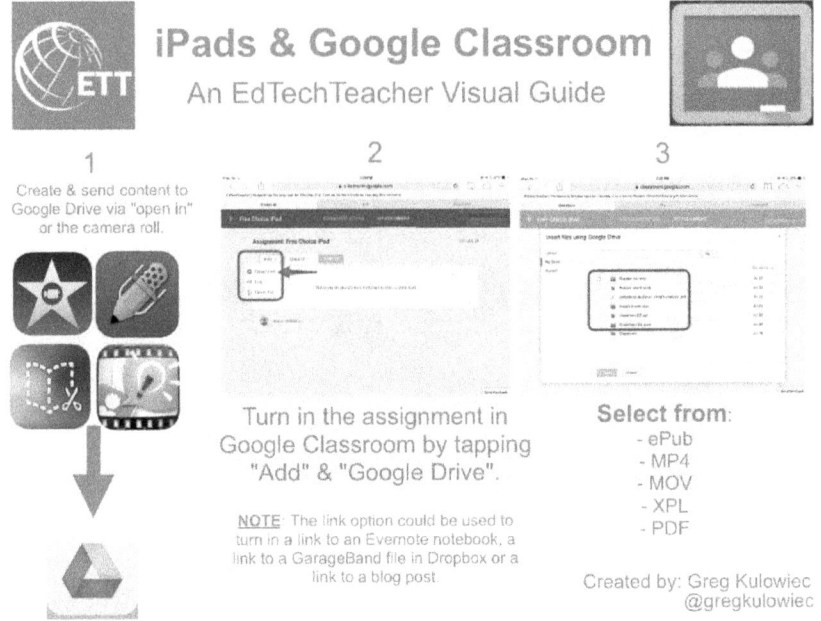

*Option 2: Student Invitations*

To personally invite students to your class, which is often viewed as the easier of the two options, you simply select the "Student" tab on the Dashboard and then select "Invite" which will allow you to search the entire student database by name (full or partial).

*Managing Classes*

Class details can be edited at any time by selecting the classroom "About" tab. This gives you the option to change the class name and description. Additionally, you can update changes in room number, class meeting time, and teacher contact information.

A great option for teachers is to upload materials from Google Drive to be attached to the main Classroom page.

Certain useful documents, such as syllabus and classroom policies, are recommended attachments for the classroom homepage. Here they are highly visible and easily accessible to students. Additionally, this helps keeps your various class documents organized and separate from each other.

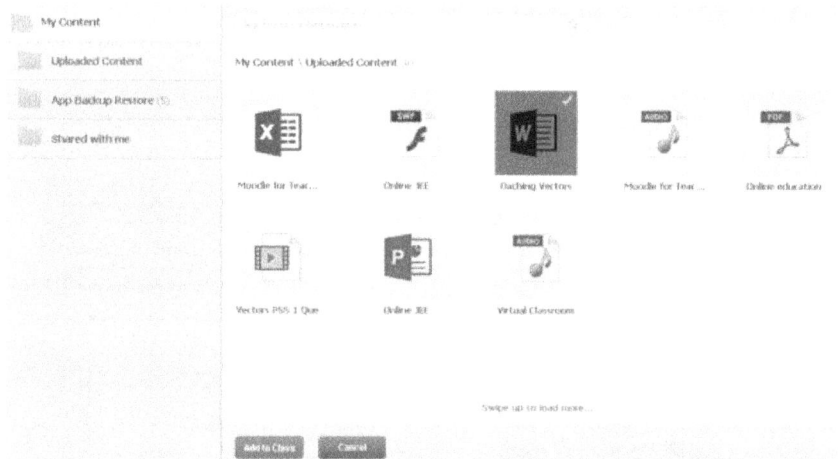

Information can be changed at any time, only by the teacher, by clicking the "About" tab followed by the "Edit" option. You can change your classroom banner here as well.

*Posting Announcements*

Once classrooms have been created the next step is to create and post announcements. These are messages that can be seen by students and parents, and can include documents,

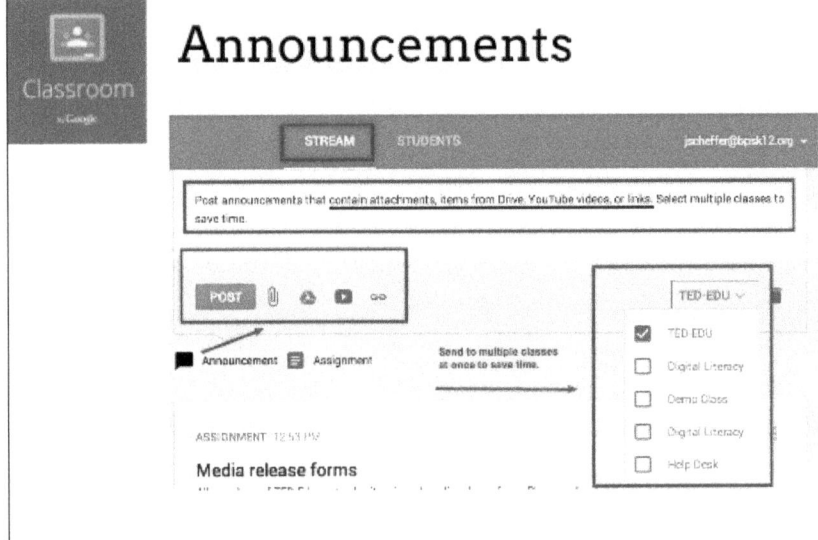

images, video files, and hyperlinks.

Announcements appear on the classroom stream in chronological order. Announcements can be simple messages such as, "Welcome to AP English, Students!" or they can contain information such as, "Please watch the video attached here and comment below on your thoughts about Climate Change."

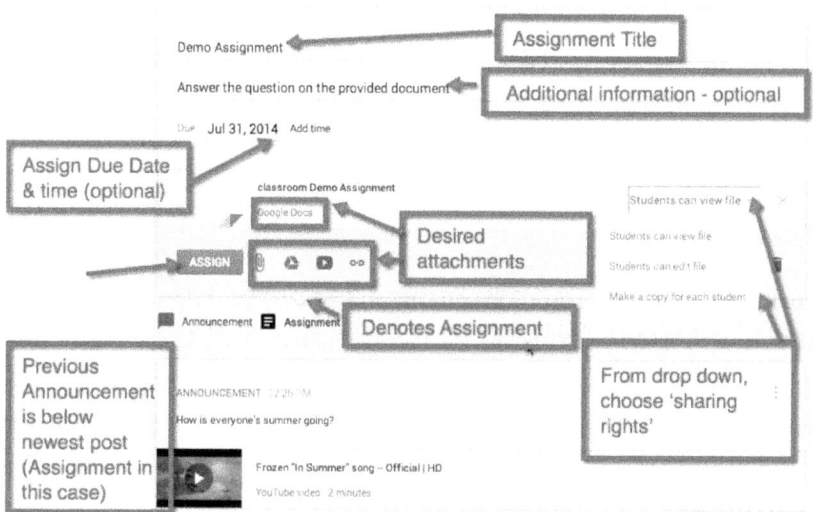

Assignments can be posted via announcements as well. There is an option to set a due date and time on assignments via the "Announcement" tab. It can be edited at any time. The default settings will automatically set as "no due date". Changing this is as simple as selecting the drop-down menu next to "no due date" and setting your preference.

To allow students to leave comments on the announcement or participate in conversations within the classroom stream, you will need to update the permission filter for each class. You have the option to approve comments before they are posted or to block students who are abusing their posting privileges.

*Creating Assignments*

When assignments are posted there are many options for the teacher to consider. Teachers control the customizability of files that are posted. This means that students must be given permission (through the assignment upload settings) to have the ability to edit files.

When an assignment is posted, there is an option to select whether the students can simply view file, view and edit file, or (now this is truly incredible) to make a copy of the file for each student. Additionally, there is an option to add assignments for multiple classes at once. This is the epitome of efficiency.

To add materials to an assignment in Google Classroom you will select "Attach," select the desired file, and then click the "Upload" button. One you see that the file has successfully uploaded, you will see a drop-down menu at the bottom of the assignment. From there, you can choose one of the following options:

- ☐ Students can view file.
- ☐ Students can edit file.
- ☐ Make a copy for each student.

The third option will create an individual copy of the document for each student and grants them editing capabilities.

*Posting Videos*

To link a YouTube video to an announcement or assignment, click the Youtube tab option (symbolized by a rounded rectangle with a small triangle inside) and select the "Video Search" option. From there, you will type keywords in the search bar and then, once you have found the video, you will click on the video itself and then select "Add." This will embed a direct link to the video in your classroom stream. You can also simply cut and paste the video URL directly into the announcement.

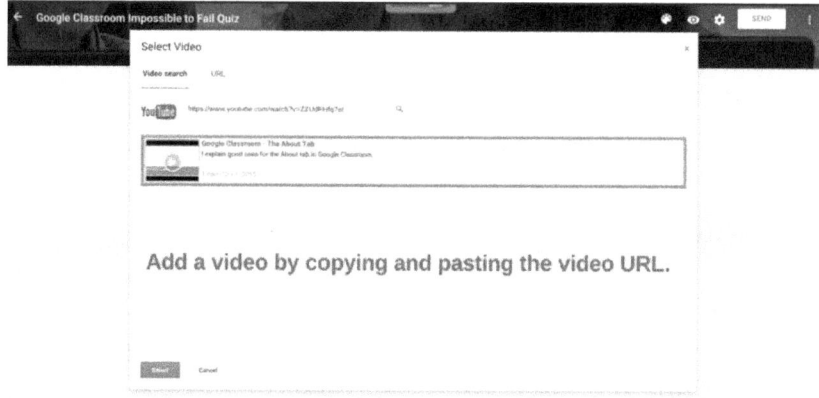

## Scheduling Due Dates

Once an assignment has been created, you will find a drop-down menu next to the "No Due Date" tab. From there you can set a date and time. If you are creating different due dates for multiple classes, set the first due date, then select additional dates and times for subsequent classes.

## Grading Assignments

If you have created an assignment copy for each student, it will appear in the "Student Work" page. From there you can comment or edit work that is in-progress or grade submitted assignments. If there is no visible file or attachment for a particular student in the class, it means that the student has yet to open the assignment, and that must be done before it can be viewed or graded by the teacher.

When viewing an assignment that is currently in-progress, there will be a number in the upper-right corner of the post which keeps track of how many students have already completed and submitted the assignment for grading. The days of walking around and checking students' notebooks are over. This is a truly innovative way to hold students accountable and keep track of multiple classes at once.

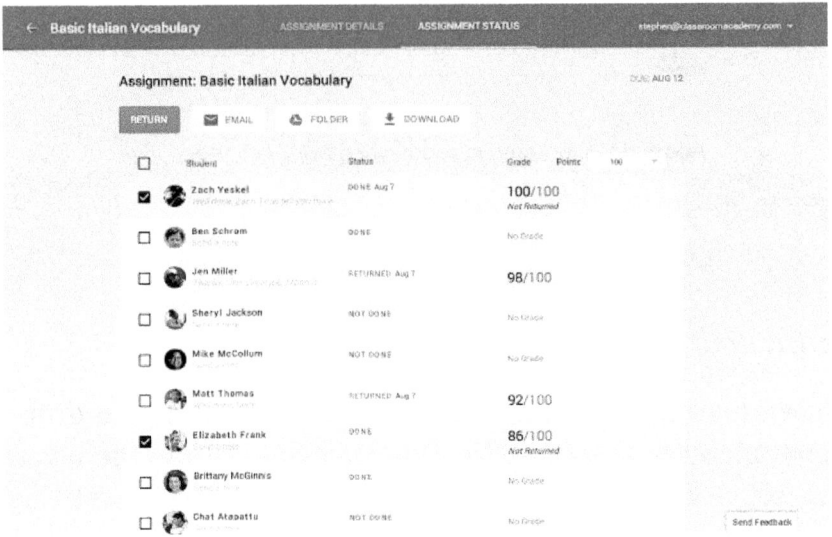

*Posting Grades*

All finalized grades can be exported to Google Sheets with ease. It is a easy as selecting the "Settings" tab (signified by a small cog in the top corner of the dashboard) and clicking "Copy All Grades to Google Sheets." The spreadsheet you create will be automatically saved to your Classroom Drive folder, where you can access it at any future time.

Grades can also be exported to a CSV (Comma Separated Values) file which is a format for viewing information in an easy-to-read table of numerical values. To create this kind of document, select the "Settings" tab and then "Download These Grades as CSV." This will download all assignment and question grades into a separate document that will also be stored in the Classroom Drive folder.

*Creating Email Groups*

Teachers within the GAFE system have an education email hosted by Gmail. This can be accessed by selecting the "Mail" tab on the top-left corner of the Google homepage. From there, select "Contacts," then "Import" student and guardian email addresses from a saved spreadsheet. You can group them into email lists, such as "AP Science Students" or "AP Science Guardians" to help organize your various contacts. This will be incredibly helpful when it comes time to creating and sending student summaries and reports (as we will cover in the next chapters).

# Chapter 3 – Practical Applications

Operating and maintaining a digital classroom is a simple process once you are aware of the incredible tools you have available. Classroom management has never been this easy and efficient!

Once you have a solid sense of the basic features available to get your digital classroom up and running, you can start to explore ways to personalize your classroom to meet your daily educational needs.

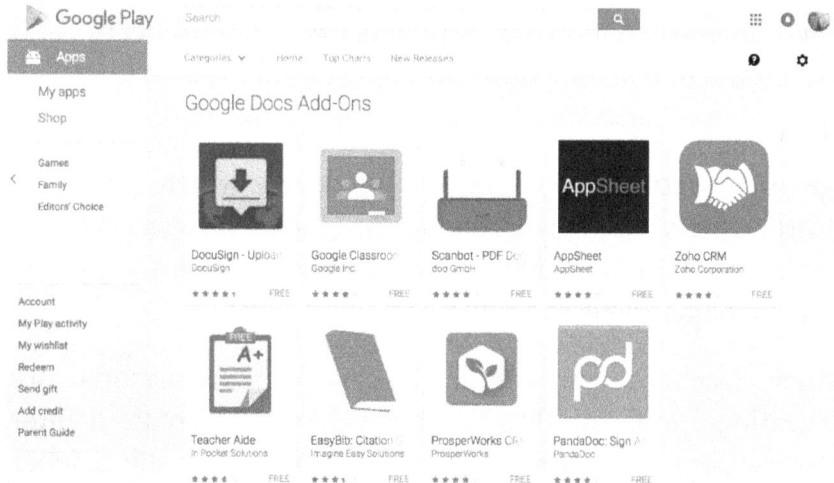

Google Classroom was designed to give teachers full control over the privacy, security, and organization of their individual classrooms. Every classroom and each individual student has their own set of unique needs. The default settings for a third-grade Science class is going to be significantly different than those necessary for a high school Health Education class.

Things to consider as a teacher include:

☐ How much freedom should students have in their public posting privileges?
☐ Which websites provide appropriate and reputable information for students to use as supplementary resources?
☐ How often do parents and guardians need to be updated on student class progress?

*Permission Settings*

With Google Classroom comment permission filters are not only available, but they are highly recommended, to apply to classroom announcement feeds and the public classroom stream. This level of security ensures that teachers maintain control over the content of the digital classroom while simultaneously allowing students to communicate and participate in conversations and information sharing.

The level of public participation depends, of course, on the age and maturity level of the students, which will vary entirely from class to class. Some teachers may prefer to disable public discussions altogether and option for private student-teacher messages instead.

Other teachers may find that public discussions are educational and enriching and can choose to create a filter that requires each comment to be approved by the teacher before being published to the classroom steam.

Google Classroom is highly customizable once you know what will work best for you and your students. If there is a privacy/sensor option that does not exist that you believe would enhance your teaching experience, please feel free to submit a suggestion to Google Classroom directly via the main website homepage at google.classroom.com.

*Managing Folders*

Teachers can compartmentalize their various classrooms with ease by creating separate folders for each class. Respective syllabi and corresponding attendance rosters can be uploaded, edited, and stored in a highly organized filing system. Grade Spreadsheets and individual class assignments can also be organized by classroom, as to enhance classroom management.

Each classroom will have its own separate dashboard, classroom stream, announcements, assignments, calendar, grades, and email groups. While the teacher has the option to duplicate and share assignments and announcements across multiple classrooms with the simple click of a button, Google Classroom makes sure to keep each classroom and its data stored entirely separate from its counterparts.

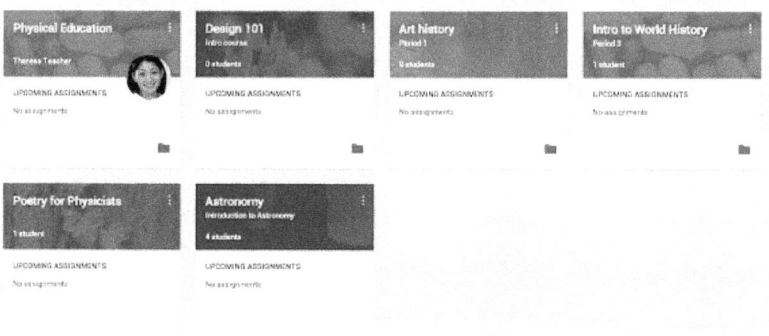

If a student is enrolled in more than one of your classes, they will have a single student file with their personal and contact information, in addition to multiple classroom folders for each class in which he or she is enrolled. This ensures that the student does not get excluded from any classroom streams or posted information.

*Calendar Share*

Google Calendar is an excellent feature that can be synced to classroom events to ensure that teachers, students, and parents all have access to important dates, school closures, events, and deadlines.

In the "Class" tab on the Google Classroom dashboard you will select the "About" tab, where you will see an option to "Open in Google Calendar." This feature allows you to create events and set due dates. Next to the calendar name is a drop-down menu. Here you will find the option to "Share this Calendar" which will make your edits visible to students and parents who have access to that particular class.

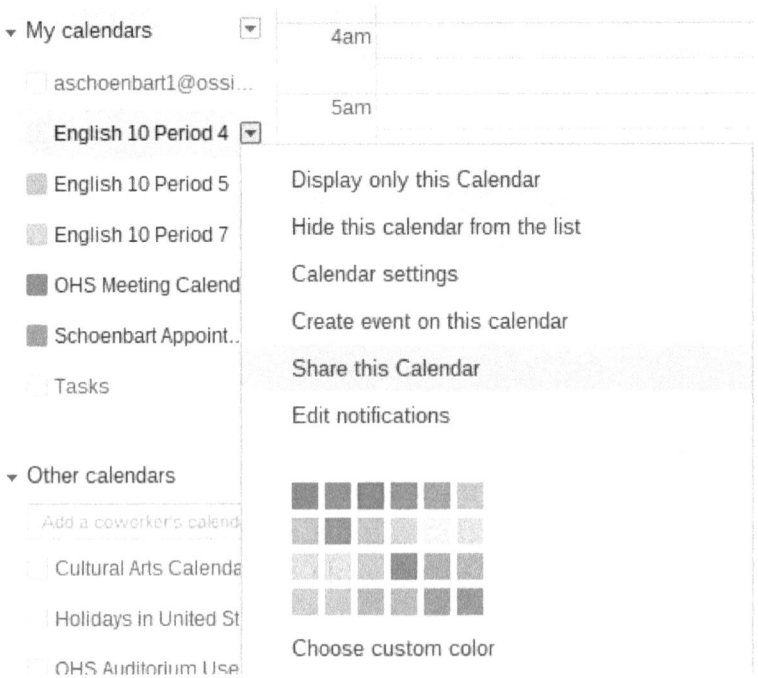

Some schools within GAFE have synchronized their school calendars to reflect administrative changes, such as snow day updates, school holidays, and large events. This takes the responsibility of posting these important dates and events to classroom calendars off of the teacher and ensures that everyone is on the same page.

## Saved Drafts

Future announcements and assignments can be created and saved as drafts until they are ready to be posted, which allows teachers to plan their lessons and schedules in advance.

To do this, simply create an announcement as described in the previous chapter, but rather than publishing immediately, select "Save as Draft". This will save the announcement and/or assignment until it is ready to be officially posted and shared with students and parents alike.

Drafts can contain files, videos, and photos. There is no limit to what can be drafted and saved for future posts. Additionally, teachers can draft group or individual emails to be saved for a later date, or to be edited later before officially sending.

Drafts are never permanent. They can always be edited or deleted. They can also be saved as a template for future posts or emails, and simply be copied and pasted into new announcements or emails as needed.

# Chapter 4 – Special Features

In addition to the basic applications available in Google Classroom, there are special features that enhance the digital classroom experience. These features are not explicitly described in most user manuals and can sometimes get lost in the mix. Here you will find the tools to customize and personalize your digital classroom in ways you never imagined before.

These particular special features aid teachers in managing their time most efficiently as well as keeping the line of communication between parents and guardians clear and open. Google Classroom is constantly updating its features to improve and maintain the highest degree of functionality, coherence, and organization.

Understanding how to use these features will help you run your classroom with ease and order. You now have all the information needed to operate and maintain the classroom of the future!

*Data Share*

Sharing data across applications is a slightly technical procedure, but also incredibly useful. For instance, if a teacher wants to share a post from the classroom stream to a social media application, or insert it into a blog post, this feature would make it as simple as the click of a button.

Google Classroom simply needs to utilize the Application Program Interface (API) which is a system of software coding that creates a link between applications.

Teachers will need to copy the particular JavaScript which will create a "Share Classroom" button that will appear in all future posts on their classroom dashboard. The script can be found by searching "Share Action Provider" for your particular phone and/or computer operating system in Google Chrome.

*Mobile Camera*

Another special feature within Google Classroom is the ability to take pictures directly through the application and attach them to posts. Note: this is a feature included in the Mobile App for Google Classroom.

To access this feature, you will create an announcement or assignment (as explained in chapter two) but this time, when you select "Add an Attachment" there will be an option to "Take Photo." Once you are satisfied with the picture, you have the option to add comments, and then, finally, select "Turn In" and it will publish the post to the dashboard stream.

*Guardian Summaries*

A recent feature on Google Classroom is "guardian email summaries" which provides information about specific students to which parents and guardians can subscribe for weekly or monthly updates. This is one way a digital classroom simplifies and enhances communication between educators and guardians concerning student needs and behavior in the classroom.

Guardian email summaries include upcoming work, missing assignments, and the particular student's class activity. By default, these summaries are turned off, but it is a very simple procedure to activate them.

An administrator must first approve and enable guardian summary capabilities for the system. Then, it is up to the teachers to invite guardians to the service. Teachers will need guardian email addresses. From there, email groups can be made, separating guardians by classroom, which will make managing the summaries much easier for the teacher.

*Topic Filters*

Creating topics for the classroom stream (which is the series of posts that appear on the dashboard in the order which they are posted) is a newly updated feature that enhances organization for teachers and students accessing the dashboard stream on a regular basis.

Topics function as an organizational filter for announcements and assignments. They can be created to reflect subject matter, class number, or whatever the teacher so chooses. For instance, if a teacher creates an announcement about a field trip, it can be organized under the topic "Trips" which would categorize it separately from announcements that are labeled as "Homework" or "News."

## Assigning Questions

One of the most recent features available to teachers is polling capabilities. This includes creating questionnaires, and multiple-choice question polls. This is an excellent feature for daily review quizzes, or simply a way to check-in with students to see how they are doing in your class.

To post a question, first select the class you would like to share the question with, then click the "Add" button on the bottom of the dashboard, followed by "Create Question." You

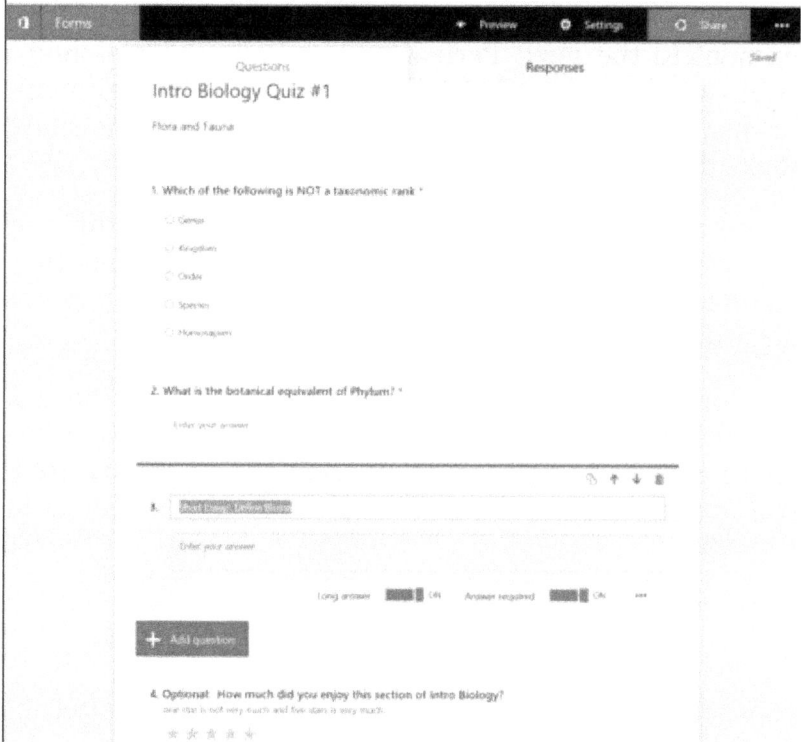

can then create a title for the question, the question itself, and select a due date from the drop-down arrow. To omit a due date, click the "X" at the top corner of the due date tab.

To post a multiple-choice question follow the same steps, but instead of the default option for "Short Answer," select the drop-down menu and change the settings to "Multiple Choice." You can create as many answer options as you would like by simply selecting "Add Option."

*Privacy Settings*

On multiple-choice questions, classmates are able to see their peers' answers as a default setting. To change the privacy settings, click the "Turn Off" button that appears under the "Summary" tab.

This is an instance of a setting that may change from one assignment to the next. Perhaps one set of multiple-choice questions is of a personal nature, or is a graded assignment. In this instance, it would be most beneficial to turn the share settings off.

However, if you are polling your students on how difficult they found an assignment or how many hours per day they spend on homework, it could be an interesting experiment to enable group share visibility settings.

The important thing to remember is that all posts have a default settings. Once you understand that you have the ability to change or remove default settings, you have total control over how your classroom operates. The power is in your hands!

## Conclusion

Google Classroom is the new gold standard for classroom management. You are fortunate to be on the frontier of redefining educational methods; paving the road for teaching professionals who follow in your footsteps. Taking the responsibility of mastering your digital classroom into your own hands is the epitome of leadership.

Now that you understand how your Google Classroom functions, it is time to experience it in a sense of a more universal application. Keep in mind that what works for everyone may not be your personal preference. Do not be afraid to be innovative with how you choose to manage your classroom. Connect with teachers around the globe who use Google Classroom and participate in a larger network of information technology. Consider your professional community exponentially expanded!

Here are some tips for you as you officially launch and maintain your virtual classroom:

- ☐ Offer assistance to parents and students who may not fully understand how to use Google Classroom.
- ☐ Ask for feedback from parents and students to ensure that communication is open and everything is functioning smoothly.
- ☐ Communicate with fellow teachers, share tips and tricks with one another for the best way to operate your online classes.
- ☐ Take full advantage of the special features that comes with Google Classroom and various other Google Educational Applications.
- ☐ Understand that you are part of a larger, universal community of educational professionals within the GAFE domain.

The more time you take to learn the ins and outs of your Google Classroom, the more efficient your classroom management will be. Knowledge is power indeed! One important factor of the technological world to keep in mind is that updates and expansions are constant.

This is a wonderful thing about participating in a digital classroom world; features are always getting better; applications are ever-expanding. The flip-side of this coin, however, is that you need to stay informed. Now that have you access to the information in this guide, in addition to the world wide web, continue learning as much as you can about your program.

Check the Google Classroom website regularly and subscribe to updates and useful information through your school email. If you choose to have the Google Classroom application on your mobile device, make sure to enable automatic updates from Google, so that you have the newest information at all times. It pays to keep up with technological changes!

As a teacher, you will want to be able to explain updates to your students and their guardians. This is an opportunity for you to pave the way for fellow educational professionals as well. Share the information you have learned and keep your eyes and ears open for ways to continue making positive changes within the profession of education!

Thank you for reading. I hope you enjoy it. I ask you to leave your honest feedback.

I think next books will also be interesting for you:

Amazon Echo

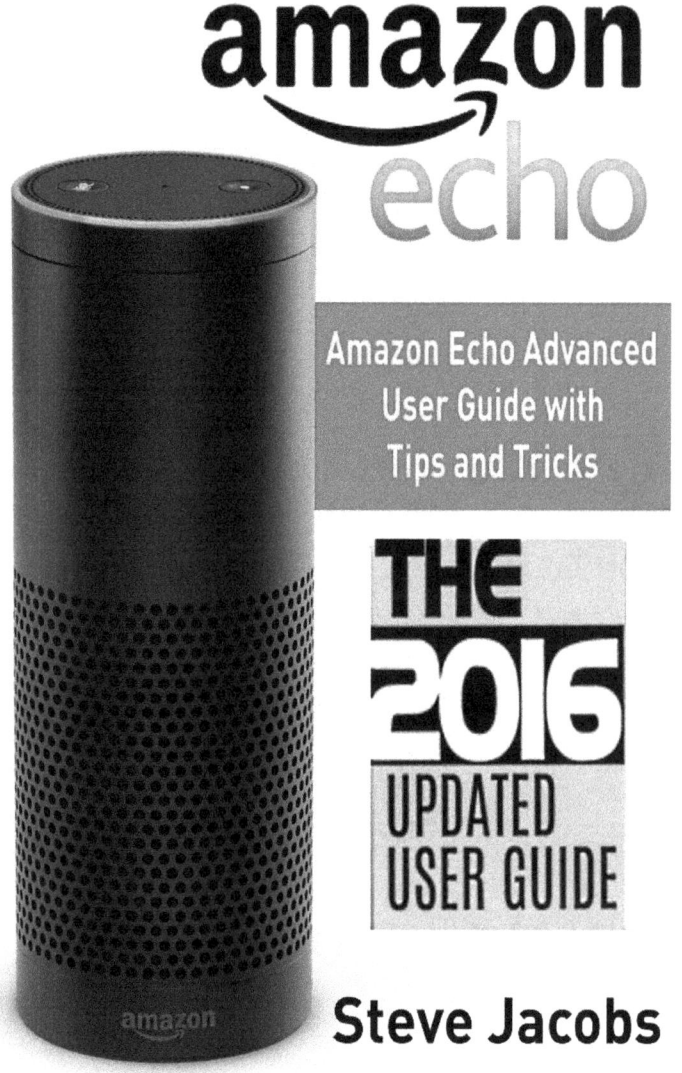

Amazon Tap

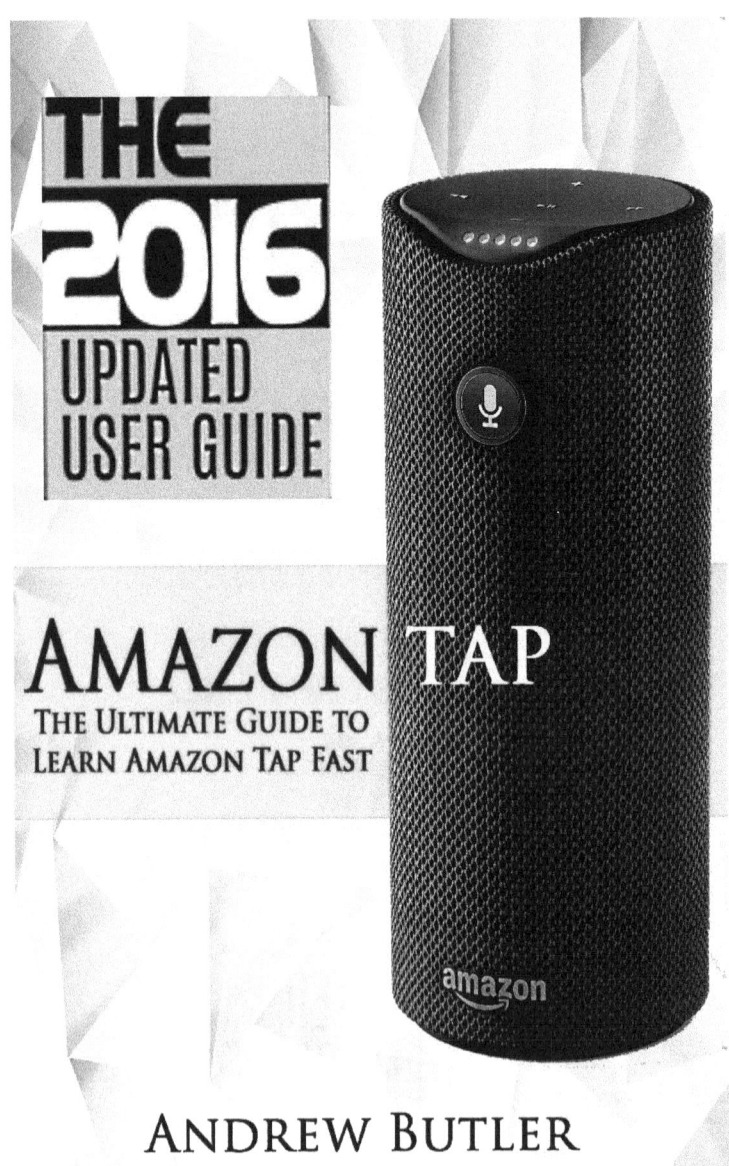

Amazon Dot

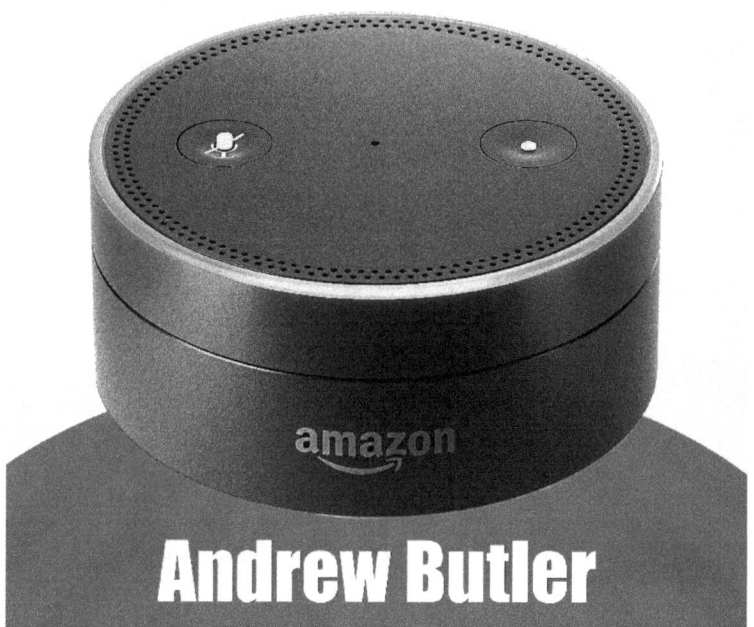

Windows 10

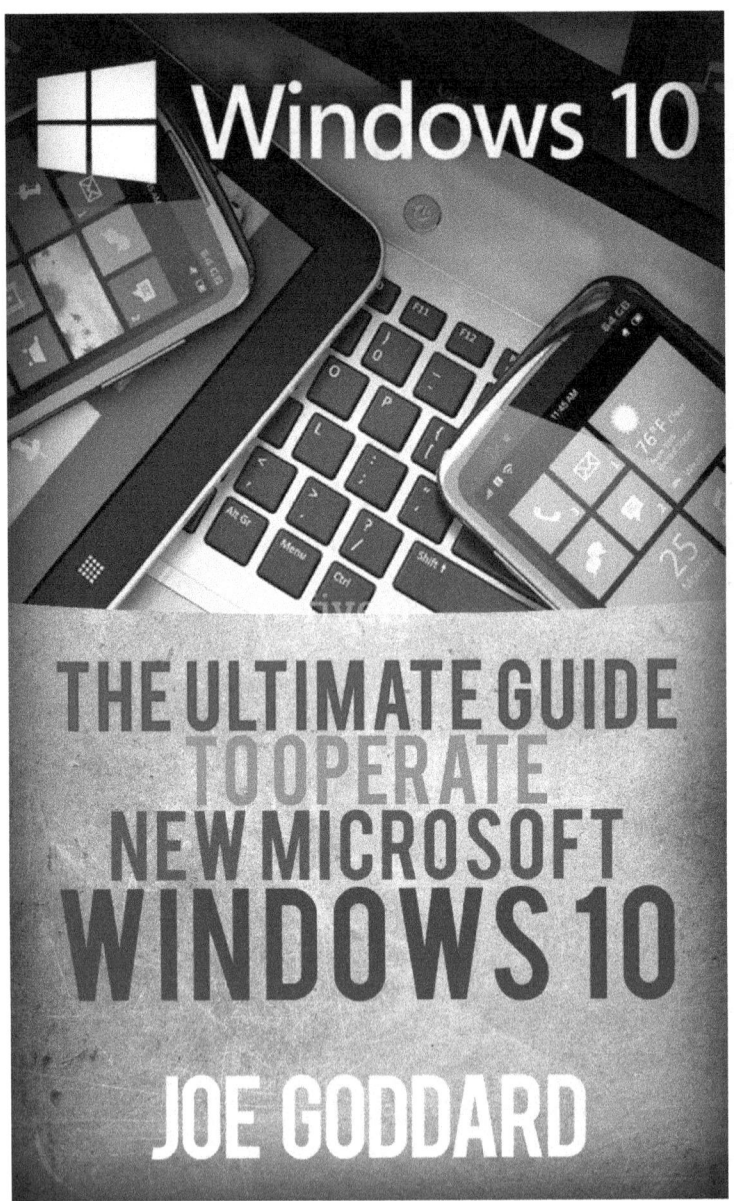

Amazon Fire TV

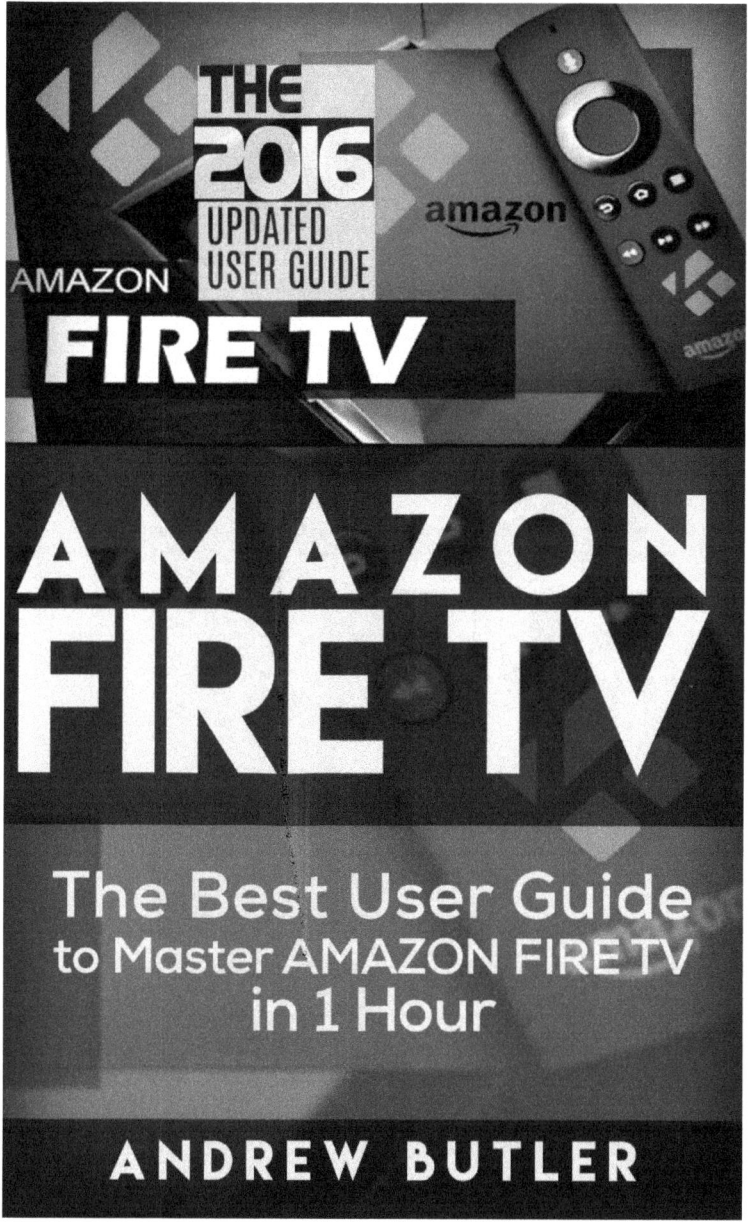

Amazon Echo

Lightning Source UK Ltd.
Milton Keynes UK
UKHW02f1839170118
316349UK00006B/483/P